SECOND WIND

THE MAGIC OF MAKING YOUR LIFE GREAT AGAIN

ROBERT MILLER

Copyright © 2020 by Robert Miller

All rights reserved.

ISBN 978-0-9975887-2-9

CUATRO CORP.
Irvine. California

ALSO BY ROBERT MILLER

Rainmaking
The Magic of Selling
C19 Economics

To Ali and Ali.

Part of you pours out of me
In these lines from time to time

A Case of You (1970)
Joni Mitchell

CONTENTS

Magic | 1

One | Health | 9

Two | Wealth | 23

Three | Happiness | 41

Bag of Tricks | 55

Wash Your Hands | 69

Inspiration | 77

My Story | 81

I don't believe in the kind of magic in my books. But I do believe something very magical can happen when you read a good book.

J. K. Rowling

YOU
have all the
MAGIC
to create the
LIFE
you want.

Magic

Believe in love. Believe in magic. Hell, believe in Santa Clause. Believe in others. Believe in yourself. Believe in your dreams. If you don't, who will.

— Jon Bon Jovi

Second Wind is a book I have planned to write for many years — perhaps as many as twenty or more. I began it when I turned fifty. I have started and stopped through the years. This time I found my second wind and completed it in ten days without looking back at my old notes.

Many marathoners believe in a concept known as **hitting the wall** which happens when an athlete depletes stored glycogen and begins feeling negative and fatigued. They believe they will hit the wall at the twenty-mile mark. A marathon is 26.2 miles and at 20 miles a marathoner must somehow find the strength to finish the race. That is the phenomenon known as a **second wind**. I hope that this book will help you find yours.

MAGIC

Many of us are close to hitting the pandemic wall — many have already hit it. America is at a tipping point. Months of "sheltering in place" and economic shutdown have severely hurt our health, finances, and emotions.

I am not going to provide a lot of detail about the pandemic and the economy here. My last book — ***C19 Economics: Your Guide to Personal and Business Finance*** — explains how we got here and what we need to do to make our nation and ourselves great again.

This is my fourth book — all my books have some magic in them because I believe in magic. ***Second Wind*** is about ***The Magic of Making Your Life Great Again***.

Let's talk about your **magic** and your **second wind**. I authored this book to help you discover your magic and catch your second wind. But you must **imagine** and **believe** that you are the magic and make it happen.

Second Wind is not a textbook. It is not a financial guide. And it is not a "self-help" book. This is a crazy and eclectic book that is written raw and unplugged. PC is not an objective or consideration— it is what it is.

MAGIC

I have completed several marathons, but never hit the wall. Quitting — or even walking or stopping — was never an option. Why? Because I was prepared physically, mentally, and emotionally. I programmed myself to finish at all costs. That is what you will do.

I can share my thoughts and experiences with you, but the rest is up to you. You — and you alone — must discover your magic and find your second wind.

How do you do that? **Imagine and believe.** **Imagine** the life you want to live — and **believe** that you can and will make it happen.

Scan once through the pages of your book and mark the parts that are of interest to you. Make notes, highlight text, and turn down page corners. It is your book and hopefully you will keep it with you for a long time.

None of us knows how long we will live. The pandemic nightmare and collateral chaos have been an unexpected wake up call. And it is a stark reminder of our human frailty and mortality. The experience is also a reminder of how strong we are, and that God gave us everything we need to survive and prosper.

MAGIC

Having reminded you of that let's focus on the future and not the past — or even the present. Let's forget about masks and gloves and social distancing and all types of germs. Instead let's be grateful for just being alive.

Here is the plan. After you have scanned through *Second Wind* get a notebook that you dedicate to your personal greatness program. Dare to be great! Imagine and believe!

As you read your book the second time begin to create your strategy for greatness. Identify your personal strengths and weaknesses. Divide your notebook into three sections: **health, wealth,** and **happiness.**

There are many techniques that you can use to make your dreams come through beyond using your notebook. Some call them tricks or hacks. Here are some of them:

Vision Board or Scrapbook
We are visual creatures and we can make our dreams come true by creating and reviewing visual images of what we want to make happen. Kind of like *Field of Dreams.* Cut and paste photos from magazines or print pictures from online sources.

MAGIC

Vision Board or Scrapbook (continued)
Your vision board (or scrapbook) does not have to be perfect. It is for "your eyes only" — unless you choose to share it. You should be creative and make your own drawings. Color outside the lines and think big.

Journal
Keep a personal journal of your thoughts and dreams and record the progress of your journey. Invest in a nicely bound hardback journal. I use the ones available online at us.moleskine.com. There is a variety of sizes available and you can have them personalized with your name or initials.

Digital File
This is my personal favorite and what I do. Buy a flash drive. I use a Samsung Bar Plus 256 GB USB 3.1 Flash Drive (available on Amazon.com). You can combine everything on your flash drive: photos, videos, music, documents, and anything else that will help you achieve your goals. In addition to the photos you take you can use some available free online on sites like Unsplash.com.

There are **thirteen magical tricks** at the back of this book in the section titled **Bag of Tricks**. There are more tips and tricks in my other three books.

MAGIC

I am going to briefly mention some sources of inspiration for this book. More sources are at the back of the book. Music is a major influence on my life, and I have included some lyrics from Joni Mitchell, Billy Idol, John Lennon, and Paul McCartney. Also included are quotes from J. K. Rowling, Andrew Weil, Joseph Conrad, Vincent Van Gough, Henry David Thoreau, Billy Idol, P. T. Barnum, Peter Lynch, Samuel Jackson, Woody Allen, Danica Patrick, Donald Trump, Richard Branson, Calvin Coolidge, Ray Bradbury, Benjamin Franklin, Audrey Hepburn, William Morris, Khalil Gibran, George Burns, Taylor Swift, Alexander Hamilton, T. S. Eliot, Oprah Winfrey, Felix the Cat, Walt Disney, Tobie Jones, L. L. Cool J, Lewis Carroll, Gordon Ramsey, Mark Zuckerberg, Wayne Gretzky, L. Frank Baum, J. M. Barrie, Ali Miller, Bob Seger, Ella Fitzgerald, and Charles Dickens. And three movies: *Coming to America*, *Shrek*, and *Caddyshack*.

My wife Ali and our daughter Ali are precious sources of love and encouragement. They provide unlimited information and inspiration for my health, wealth, and happiness. I have increasingly learned to take their advice to keep me "forever young".

MAGIC

I have always been fascinated by magic. When I was in kindergarten there was a magic shop near my school, that I would stop at after school.

When I arrived home, I would sit in front of the little black and white television screen and watch the black and white cat with the big grin. Felix had his bag of tricks which helped him get out of one mess after another and I started learning my own tricks.

The first time my family went to Disneyland (on opening day) I was fascinated to see all the characters from the fairy tales my parents and grandmothers had read me — and I have always believed in fantasy and magic. I hope that you will discover the magic within you and that it will help make your dreams come true.

Thanks for reading *Second Wind*. May God protect you and yours. And may you use your magic to make your life great again.

Robert Miller
Irvine, California
August 8, 2020

Nothing
is more important in
Your Life
than
Your Health

ONE
Health

He who has health has hope; and he who has hope has everything.

— Arabian proverb

Each of us has our own prescription for health. Sadly, many us fail to follow our prescriptions. Your personal health strategy should take into consideration three aspects: your body, your mind, and heart and soul — your spirit.

Investing in your health must be your primary investment. Remember that longevity is one thing and quality of life is another. Living to 100 means nothing if you are suffering from aches and pains because you did not respect your body and mind.

Who wants to be in a nursing home unable to wash your own hands for lunch that you probably do not even want to eat anyway? It may not be too late to avoid that.

Your health should be your biggest investment.

Health

1 | Body | 13

2 | Mind | 17

3 | Heart, Soul, and Life | 19

SPEED
STRENGTH
STAMINA
STRETCH

1
BODY

The bottom line is that the human body is complex and subtle, and oversimplifying — as common sense sometimes impels us to do — can be hazardous to your health.

— Andrew Weil

We only have one body in our lifetime and we have the responsibility to do everything within our power to build and protect it.

Let me share how I take care of my body. You may or may not choose to follow my lead, but these things work for me. I do everything I can to ensure that my quality of life is the best that it can be. I want to stay out of assisted living and free from all diseases. I do not want to be somewhere watching *I Love Lucy* reruns — not knowing who I am or where I am — and not recognizing anyone but Lucy and Ricky. When we lose control of our minds and bodies, we will lose our independence

BODY

My nutritional program is plant-based and what you might call vegan — mostly raw vegan. 100% raw may not always be practical so I incorporate some cooked foods in my diet. Those include baked sweet potatoes, squashes, lightly steamed vegetables, and some baked goods.

I do not consume any animal products and everything I eat, or drink is organic, gluten-free, or soy-free. I avoid prepared and packaged foods and drinking water that is bottled in plastic. Imitation meats are not for me. I drink hot and cold decaffeinated teas.

Design your personal nutritional program to include lots of fresh raw organic salads with creative home-made dressings — and add lots of things like pickles, olives, capers, and beans like garbanzos — season creatively.

Try to consume copious amounts of lightly steamed organic vegetable like carrots, celery, onions, potatoes, broccoli, cauliflower, and squash. There are all types of squashes you can bake — brushed with coconut oil and seasoned as you like. You can make raw soups in your blender — or cooked soup made with organic vegetable base.

BODY

If you are concerned about getting enough protein you can source it from beans cooked alone or added to your salads. Or you can make your own signature flavored hummus from garbanzo beans. Some vegetables are a reliable source of protein. And you can make lots of dishes with quinoa.

Shakes and smoothies can be delicious ways to consume protein — add raw vegan proteins. You can add a limited amount of fresh or frozen fruits and raw greens like spinach and kale. Supplement your shakes and smoothies with raw coconut and chia seeds and flavor with raw cacao.

Eat a lot of fresh and frozen fruits but limit the ones which contain a high sugar content. Apples and berries are reliable sources of nutrients. Stay away from high-sugar fruits. If you juice at home use a vegetable base and supplement with low-glycemic fruits only.

We use a Blendtec® blender and an Omega® slow masticating juicer. Make sure your pots pans, utensils, and containers are nontoxic — use stainless steel and avoid Teflon and other coatings. Invest a few hours to make sure that you get rid of toxins in your kitchen.

BODY

The key to your nutritional program is pureness and variety. Think nutrient-rich plant-based foods as close to nature as possible. That does not mean packaged processed foods that try to mislead you by printing "natural" on the label. Arsenic is natural and can be organic — and can be labeled vegan, gluten, and non-GMO, etc.

Those of you addicted to fast foods and junk foods and who are voracious carnivores should avoid trying to dramatically modify your diet "cold turkey" (excuse the pun). Transition from the foods and beverages you plan to phase out slowly — and realistically introduce the foods and beverages you want to phase in at a comfortable pace.

There is no reason for you to starve yourself. Eating well requires a big commitment but the benefits to your wellness, longevity, and quality of life are limitless and priceless.

Supplements are highly controversial and can be expensive. It you choose to supplement your diet use only pure, high-quality products. Do not buy "Made in China" supplements which may contain toxins. Know your sources. Seek professional advice.

BODY

The other half of caring for your body is your exercise program. These days most people are avoiding public gyms, and many are afraid of going outdoors to exercise. So here is my own in-home fitness routine.

My cardio exercise in done on my Bellicon® Mini-Trampoline. There are a lot of mini-trampoline workout routines on YouTube. Bouncing is low-impact and the possibilities and benefits are unlimited.

I use dumbbells and kettlebells for strength and bodybuilding. Medicine balls can be used in a variety of ways. There are many stretching exercises for flexibility.

Do not allow your body to weaken and do not let your muscles atrophy. It is never too late to take control of your body — recapture your physical fitness and protect it with a daily routine. You should seek professional help to develop a safe and effective fitness program which includes both diet and exercise.

Plan and commit. Pace yourself. You can not go from zero to sixty overnight, but you can get started now on the road to feeling and looking "forever young."

OUR MINDS ARE THE WORLD'S MOST AMAZING COMPUTERS

2
MIND

The mind of man is capable of anything.

— Joseph Conrad

Once we lose our ability to control our minds we might as well be dead. Many of us fail to recognize the value of growing our minds and protecting our mental health.

Staying forever young is just as dependent on feeding and exercising your mind as it is caring for your body. The adage "use it or lose it" equally applies to both.

Both of my parents and both grandmothers suffered from some form of dementia in their later years. I do everything that I can to keep my mind strong and alert. Break some rules. Go crazy! Acting a little crazy may keep you from going insane. Have fun. Live every moment to the max. And wash your hands for lunch.

CONNECT YOUR
MIND,
BODY,
HEART,
SOUL,
AND
LIFE.

3
HEART, SOUL AND LIFE

I put my heart and my soul into my work, and I have lost my mind in the process.

— Vincent Van Gough

Corazón, alma, y vida is Spanish for **heart, soul, and life**. This is the most important chapter in this book. Unless you can break the code on connecting your **Body, Mind, Heart, Soul, and Life** it will be difficult for you to recapture and protect your health, wealth, and happiness.

Seabiscuit was a thoroughbred who suffered an injury that almost ended his racing career. Seabiscuit did not look like a champion. He was relatively small and knobby-kneed. Many felt he was too laid-back. Because he had *heart* the little horse trained physically and mentally and made an amazing comeback winning the legendary Santa Anita Handicap in 1940. Seabiscuit knew he was a champion and that is all that mattered. Have **heart**.

Each of us has our own definition of wealth.

—

What is yours?

TWO
Wealth

It doesn't matter about money; having it, not having it. Or having clothes, or not having them. You're still alone with yourself in the end.

— Billy Idol

For many, America is synonymous with wealth. **The American Dream** has been compromised by China's attack on the United States and by the current blood on the streets of our cities. That attack threatens our nation's "life, liberty, and pursuit of happiness."

There are many components of wealth and everyone has their own unique perception and definition of wealth. You may never have a better opportunity to build and protect great wealth. The pandemic has created a "perfect storm" of economic opportunity. Everything you need to get started on your road to millions is here — just add your own magic.

The man is richest
whose pleasures and cheapest.

Henry David Thoreau

Wealth

4 | Income | 27

5 | Investments | 29

6 | Retirement | 31

7 | Insurance | 33

8 | Real Estate | 35

9 | Business | 37

10 | Legacy | 39

TRUE WEALTH
REQUIRES
MULTIPLE
STREAMS OF
INCOME

4
INCOME

True economy always consists of making the income exceed the out-go.

— P. T. Barnum

Unless you have unlimited wealth and know exactly how long you are going to live you need to have multiple streams of income.

For most people who are not yet retired the primary source of income is earned income from a job — an employee for somebody else or for their own company. Their earned income is reported to the IRS on a W-2 or 1099 form. Unless you have a gigantic salary, it is difficult to build wealth solely through earned income. Business owners may have additional income from distribution of profits.

Real estate income can be passive or active depending on whether you manage the properties yourself. Create multiple streams.

INVESTING
IS NOT AS EASY AS YOU MAY THINK
GET HELP

5
INVESTMENTS

Know what you own, and know why you own it.

— Peter Lynch

The world of investments is extremely complex and is one in which you should avoid making costly mistakes just because you do not want to pay for professional help.

The relationship between risk and return is known as the **risk/reward ratio. ROI** (return on investment) measures performance and is used to evaluate efficiency of investments or to compare different investments or classes of investments.

Successful investing demands skill, talent, time, experience, capital, and disciplined. Unless you have these, you should seek the advice of an experienced advisor. Beware of multilevel investment plans.

RETIREMENT
CAN BE
HEAVEN
OR IT CAN BE
HELL

6
RETIREMENT

It is better to live rich than to die rich.

— Samuel Johnson

What is your vision of retirement? Do you have a strategy? When are you planning to retire — and what do you plan to do?

You will need more to finance your retirement than Social Security income. You may find yourself in big trouble if you are counting on Social Security and/or a company pension.

If you have a qualified retirement plan this is the time to have it reviewed by a retirement specialist. Remember that means more than someone just having an insurance and/or securities license. They need experience.

Invest in finding someone who is licensed, has a clean record, has more than ten years of experience and can provide many options.

There are worse things in life than death. Have you ever spent an evening with an insurance salesman?

Woody Allen

7
Insurance

Driving race cars is risky; not having life insurance is riskier.

— Danica Patrick

Insurance — for some — triggers the same negative emotions as dentists and canned spinach. The fact is that insurance should be at the base of every strategy for health, wealth, and happiness.

Insurance has always played a critical role in the economy providing many ways to build and protect wealth.

The pandemic's devastating economic impact should serve as a reminder that individuals, businesses, and governments could have mitigated some of the losses. The net effect of the pandemic will be an increase in sales of insurance products as well as an increase of premiums caused by additional policy claims and payouts.

Real Estate
CAN BE YOUR ROAD TO
MILLIONS

8
REAL ESTATE

It's tangible, it's solid, it's beautiful. It's artistic, from my standpoint, and I just love real estate.

— Donald Trump

Real estate investing has traditionally been a buffer against riskier investments and real estate will continue to serve that purpose. Buyers and sellers have slowed down their timing but will be back in the game as the economy opens.

Before the crisis paralyzed America, the housing market faced a supply shortage. Although economic uncertainty and social distancing have negatively impacted home sales the hit to home prices may be delayed and is highly unpredictable. The residential real estate market should continue to benefit from low mortgage rates. Asian buyers will continue to fade away and will be replaced by others. There are fortunes to be made.

After all, the chief business of the American people is business. They are profoundly concerned with producing, buying, selling, investing and prospering in the world.

Calvin Coolidge

9
BUSINESS

Business opportunities are like buses, there's always another one coming.

— Richard Branson

Business ownership offers you the most potential for creating great wealth. And in addition to making money owning a business has other advantages. But it is not as easy as it sounds. It can be a road to heaven or to hell depending on you.

If you are already a business owner, you may be facing the greatest challenges or have access to tremendous opportunities. Many great fortunes are made in the worst of times. This is when you need to evaluate every aspect of your business, make a plan which is both realistic and agile, and take immediate steps not only to survive but to prosper during and after the pandemic. If you are not currently a business owner, you may want to invest in one passively or actively.

It doesn't matter what you do, he said, so long as you change something from the way it was before you touched it into something that's like you after you take your hands away. The difference between the man who just cuts lawns and a real gardener is in the touching, he said. The lawn-cutter might just as well not have been there at all; the gardener will be there a lifetime.

Ray Bradbury
Fahrenheit 451

10
LEGACY

If you would not be forgotten as soon as you are dead, either write something worth reading or do something worth writing.

— Benjamin Franklin

The legacy you leave does not necessarily have to be just about money. Although that is the focus of most legacies there are other things you may want to leave your family and society when you die.

The first thing you must do right away is to get a living trust so that you can avoid probate, provide for your family, and make sure that your wishes are carried out when you die.

Your trust must be properly funded with your assets. Do not cut corners with your trust because by the time it is discovered that there is a problem you may be dead. This step is absolutely mandatory for everyone.

The most important thing is to enjoy your life — to be happy. It's all that matters.

Audrey Hepburn

THREE
HAPPINESS

The true secret of happiness lies in the taking a genuine interest in all the details of daily life.

— William Morris

The People's Republic of China has long been referred to as "the land of ping-pong, pandas, and human rights violations." The recent actions of the CCP has robbed happiness from people around the globe for years to come.

Discover your magic, catch your second wind, and recover and protect your happiness now. The best way to do that is to simply invest a few hours to spell out your own definition of happiness. Is it the Rolex Air-King or the Bombardier Challenger? The Mercedes-Benz or the BMW? Facebook likes? Instagram followers?

Or **love, family,** and **passion**?

Rolex Air-King
$6,450

Bombardier Challenger
$32,000,000

Happiness
Priceless

Happiness

11 | Love | 45

12 | Family | 47

13 | Relationships | 49

14 | Belief | 51

15 | Passion | 53

All you need is love
All you need is love
All you need is love, love
Love is all you need

All You Need Is Love (1967)
John Lennon and Paul McCartney

11
LOVE

Life without love is like a tree without blossoms or fruit.

— Khalil Gibran

What is most important to you — being in love or being loved? Love can be confusing. Who really knows what love is? How important is love to you?

They say love makes the world go around. Love is illusive to some — fatal to others. I have only been in love once in my life and it has lasted over forty years.

We all know there are many assorted flavors of love from puppy love to a fiery romance. You must wonder what went wrong when someone talks about their "ex" — or complains that they went through a "nasty" divorce. Have you ever heard someone talk about a "wonderful" divorce? If love is more than flowers and candy what is it?

Happiness is having large, loving, close-knit family in another city.

George Burns

12
Family

Family is not an important thing, it's everything.

— Michael J. Fox

I would like to tell you that I had a happy family life growing up but I did not. Love and family were two things that I wanted which never happened for me as a child.

My father never told me he loved me until the last years of his life. My mother's love was conditional — based on her wants and needs. My maternal grandmother's love was very manipulative. Unconditional love was something that I did not get.

My family was as dysfunctional as it could have been. The environment was toxic with nonstop arguing. I am grateful for everything my parents did for me — the love I never realized but they probably intended. I loved them dearly from the bottom of my heart.

Relationships are more than Facebook friends and Instagram followers. Most of the relationships in our lives come and go like the wind.

13
RELATIONSHIPS

You have people come into your life shockingly and surprisingly. You have losses that you never thought you'd experience. You have rejection and you have to learn how to deal with that and how to get up the next day and go on with it.

— Taylor Swift

Relationships include friends and lovers — business associates — and social media connections. Having 5,000 Facebook friends and 30,000 LinkedIn connections really does not mean much. I would trade all of those for just one devoted friend.

Like love, relationships can be amazingly wonderful and fulfilling — or they can be toxic and draining. The older I become the more vigilant I am about both personal and business relationships. Tay Tay says it all — people come and go — get used to it.

What else do you believe in beside that the sun will come up tomorrow?

14
BELIEF

Those who stand for nothing fall for anything.

— Alexander Hamilton

What are your beliefs and why? Belief is at the core of our souls and directly affects our happiness. Do you believe in a higher being — or that you evolved from a simple amoeba? Do you believe in extraterrestrials?

My favorite quote is from *Peter Pan*:

The moment you doubt whether you can fly, you cease forever to be able to do it.

Believe in yourself. Trust yourself. That may be the most powerful secret to catching your second wind. Believe you can catch your second wind and you will. Do not buy into the fear that you might hit the wall. Unless you believe there is a wall you will never hit it.

It is obvious that we can no more explain a passion to a person who has never experienced it than we can explain light to the blind.

T. S. Eliot

15
PASSION

Passion is energy. Feel the power that comes from focusing on what excites you.

— Oprah Winfrey

Passion moves the world. For me life is all about passion. It is about living life with purpose. It is about making the biggest possible impact on society and the lives of others every day.

Let's remember Seabiscuit — that little racehorse with **heart**. Passion drives us to fame and fortune — and it can destroy us.

What are your passions and how passionate are you? Passion cannot be bought. Passion cannot be acquired. Either you have passion in your gut, or you do not. Passion is the "x-factor" that makes life worth living. Combined with belief passion makes dreams come true. They all go together — your love, family, relationships, belief, and passion.

When I'm driving in my car
And that man comes on the radio
And he's telling me more and more
About some useless information
Supposed to fire my imagination

(I Can't Get No) Satisfaction
Rolling Stones
Mick Jagger and Keith Richards (1965)

BAG OF TRICKS

We sure outfoxed them.

— Felix the Cat

Felix the Cat, created as a cartoon character in the silent film era, has innate human traits, emotions, and intentions — and is a Master of Psychology and gamesmanship.

The surrealistic situations that Felix faced are much like what we are going through now. The iconic cat with his black body, white face, enormous eyes, and big grin gets out of one mess after another.

Felix always carried his 'Magic Bag of Tricks' that he used to outfox his opponents.

IMAGINE

1
IMAGINE

I hope that we never lose sight of one thing — that it all started with a mouse.

— Walt Disney

Imagine yourself as the person you used to be — or the person that you have always wanted to be. It is all up to use. Use your tricks to make all of our dreams come true.

Imagination is vital to the success of capitalism. Whatever we can imagine we can find a way to create. America was virtually built through imagination. People from all over the world arrived here imagining a life of freedom and prosperity.

Our New Economy will be created through the imaginations of those of those who have come before us. Imagine!

2
BE EXTRAORDINARY

The thing about Hitchcock which is quite extraordinary for a director of that time, he had a very strong sense of his own image and publicizing himself. Just a very strong sense of himself as the character of Hitchcock.

— Toby Jones

Being "extraordinary" does not mean being a contrarian, weird or eccentric. It does not mean wearing pink ties (although there's nothing wrong with that) or loud plaid suits (no comment).

How then can you be extraordinary? Like the chicken and the egg, the question might be whether you are born extraordinary or become extraordinary. It really does not matter. Those who are extraordinary in the new economy will create tremendous wealth.

3
SUPERSIZE YOUR DREAMS

I started out mopping the floor just like you guys. But now... now I'm washing lettuce. Soon I'll be on fries; then the grill. And pretty soon, I'll make assistant manager, and that's when the big bucks start rolling in.

— Maurice (Louie Anderson)
Coming to America (1988)

Always supersize or "Go Big." Always. And all dreams are relative. We all have them, and they come and go during our lifetimes. Hold on tight to your dreams — all of them.

In 2007 Donald Trump published "Think Big and Kick Ass: In Business and in Life". Obviously thinking big worked for Donald Trump and it can work for you.

What does "supersize your dreams" mean to you?

4
TRUST WHO YOU ARE

After a while, you learn to ignore the names people call you and just trust who you are.

— Shrek (Mike Myers)
Shrek (2001

The more you do or try to do the more people will trash talk about you. Fuggedaboutit! It does not matter. If you did not learn anything else during this shutdown you should have learned "not to sweat the small stuff" and that it's all small stuff.

Trust who you are. Believe unequivocally in yourself. That does not mean that you should be an arrogant narcissistic psychopath, but you must believe in yourself and your vision. Wherever you find spiritual strength, rely on that to constantly remind yourself who you are and why you get up each day. Make every moment of your life count.

5
STAY FOCUSED

Stay focused, go after your dreams and keep moving toward your goals.

— L L Cool J

Veteran race car drivers quickly learn that they must always keep the "peddle to the metal' no matter what happens on the track. When rookie drivers see an accident on the course, they automatically lift their feett off of the accelerator pedals out of a sense of self-preservation. It's a natural reflex.

When champion drivers see something horrible on the course, they put their feett down harder because they know that most of the other drivers will be lifting theirs.

Seabiscuit and other thoroughbreds act as if they are wearing blinders. Do not let anything get between you and the finish line. Winning is an attitude not an event.

6
CREATE YOUR OWN WORLD

If I had a world of my own, everything would be nonsense. Nothing would be what it is, because everything would be what it isn't. And, contrary wise, what is, it wouldn't be. And, what is wouldn't be, it would. You see?

— *Alice*
Alice's Adventure in Wonderland (1865)
Lewis Carroll

When you think about it we all create our own individual worlds every day. Create a wonderful world of opportunity, challenge, and achievement. Create your own world of wealth, health, and happiness.

Hopefully after you study these 13 Magic Tricks you will know who you are and what you are doing and WHY. The world you create can be beautiful or ugly. It can be fantasy or reality. Choose!

7
LOOK FOR THE NEXT COW

I don't like looking back. I'm always constantly looking forward. I'm not the one to sit and cry over spilt milk. I'm too busy looking for the next cow.

— Gordon Ramsey

Always be looking to the next deal. Do not permanently attach yourself to anything or anybody. Marriages are for romantic relationships and not for business.

Be quick to forget about the past — and quick to move on. Especially now there are so many deals and clients that you have choices — lots of them. And there are going to be increasingly more as the economy opens.

Create an optimal DEAL SHEET and stay on the outlook for any deals that may match your parameters. Remain open minded.

8
TAKE RISKS

The biggest risk is not taking any risk… In a world that's changing really quickly, the only strategy that is guaranteed to fail is not taking risks.

— Mark Zuckerberg

After Mark Zuckerberg's warning about managing your reputation do not let anything keep you from taking risks. Make one of your mottos "nothing ventured, nothing gained."

There are frivolous risks and there are calculated risks. Frivolous risks are based on emotions and calculated risks are based on reason. Most risks involve a combination of both in varying proportions.

Our lives program us to be risk adverse. As toddlers learning to walk, we have a natural tendency to stand up when we stumble.

9
BE WHERE THE PUCK IS GOING

I skate to where the puck is going to be, not where it has been.

— Wayne Gretzky

"The Great One" always skates to where the puck is going. Be like the great one. You do not want to be where the puck is and especially not where the puck was. Be where the puck is going.

Unless you believe in psychic readers, mediums, and crystal balls the coming weeks, months and years will probably be the most challenging of our lifetimes.

Forget about traditional fundamental and technical analysis. Dramatically change the way you think. Stop acting entirely logically and start increasingly acting based on your feelings about where the puck is going.

10
STOP FOLLOWING RULES

You don't learn to walk by following rules. You learn to walk by doing, and by falling over.

— Richard Branson

Like badges, we don't need no stinkin' rules. Stop following rules. Challenge rules. The only rules are that there are no rules.

Obviously, there are some rules that you should follow like stopping at a red light and paying your taxes. But most other rules are roadblocks to your success.

You have the freedom to determine exactly which rules you choose to follow — and exactly which rules you choose to challenge or ignore. Push against rules and push as hard as you can to constantly redefine them.

11
BE A CINDERELLA STORY

Cinderella story. Outta nowhere. A former greenskeeper, now, about to become the Masters champion. It looks a miracle... It's in the hole! It's in the hole! It's in the hole!

— Carl Spackler (Bill Murray)
Caddyshack (1980)

Almost everyone loves a "Cinderella Story." We love *Beauty and the Beast, Harry Potter, The Wizard of Oz, Alice in Wonderland,* and *Peter Pan.* What is our favorite land in Disneyland? Most of us love Fantasyland.

Make your life a fairy tale. Make it a Cinderella Story. Create your Pumpkin Coach and ride it to the most exciting and prosperous place it can take you. It is easy. All you must do is dream and believe. Reach for the stars — all of them and always wash your hands for lunch.

12
BE BRAVE

'You have plenty of courage, I am sure,' answered Oz. 'All you need is confidence in yourself. There is no living thing that is not afraid when it faces danger. The true courage is in facing danger when you are afraid, and that kind of courage you have in plenty.'

— L. Frank Baum
The Wonderful Wizard of Oz (1900)

What is courage? Unlike charisma which is a priceless gift from God courage can be acquired. How do we build courage in our lives? We build courage from pain, hurt, and failing. The more we stumble the more we need courage to get back up. But courage comes from our guts and not our minds.

13
BELIEVE

The moment you doubt whether you can fly, you cease for ever to be able to do it.

— J.M. Barrie
Peter Pan (1904)

This is the most amazing strategy. It is very simple but extremely difficult to achieve. We all know the story of the four-minute mile. We know the story of the Wright Brothers and their quest for manned flight. But many of us choose to be doubters and haters instead of simply just believing.

Jules Verne believed in going to the moon and journeying under the sea. He believed in travelling around the world in eighty days. Walt Disney believed in his little mouse. Steve Jobs believed in his computer. Elon Musk believes. So does every successful entrepreneur — the unsuccessful ones stopped believing somewhere along the road.

WASH YOUR HANDS

I love daddy…!
I remember when he was super happy.

— Ali Miller

In 1967 The Beatles sang about love in "All You Need Is Love" (by John Lennon and Paul McCartney) and love may be all we need to get through this pandemic.

There is nothing you can know that isn't known
Nothing you can see that isn't shown
There's nowhere you can be that isn't where
    you're meant to be
It's easy

CONNECT WITH ROBERT
RobertMillerNow@Gmail.com
Facebook.com/RobertMillerNow
LinkedIn.com/In/RobertMillerNow
Instagram.com/RobertMillerNow
Twitter.com/RobertMillerNow
RobertMillerNow.com

WASH YOUR HANDS

When our daughter was in kindergarten the happiest time of the day was lunchtime when the kids could run outside to the playground and play. Her teacher would yell "Wash your hands for lunch." and the fun began.

Not long before America's last economic meltdown leading to the Great Depression my life was out of balance. I was working sixteen or more hours a day and rarely saw my wife and our daughter Ali. One day Ali sent me this email:

I love daddy...! I remember when he was super happy.

You were so crazy and fun... remember yelling: "Wash your hands for lunch" going to San Diego and picking up the shells? Spending hundreds of dollars at Dave & Busters?

HAHA and the race cars... remember the race cars? We would race!

What about the times we went to Knott's Berry Farm to pick out geodes and you would get me those princess caps and we would pan for gold and go on the Dinosaur Ride?

WASH YOUR HANDS

Remember making messes at the restaurants with Tim & Patsy...? HAHA

That was so much fun, you were always so happy... and crazy, get crazy again... I like it when you are funny and crazy... like Dennis the Menace all grown up... that's how I remember you when I was little... like the really big kid... who was also really smart, always knew what to do, and took the best care of me no matter what!

I love you more than... what? The whole world! Do you remember when I first told you that after we left grandma and grandpa's? You were shocked... you said...

"really? More than the whole world?" HAHA And I said: "yes daddy, more than the WHOLE WORLD!" DADDY be crazy! DADDY ON THE LOOSE.

WASH YOUR HANDS FOR LUNCH!

As I publish *C19 Second Wind* America is six months into the pandemic nightmare. For a while now it has seemed like every day is just another day out of the movie *Ground Hog Day* (1993). I want some days like Phil (Bill Murray) talked about: "I was in the Virgin Islands once. I met a girl. We ate lobster and

WASH YOUR HANDS

drink piña coladas. At sunset we made love like sea otters. THAT was a pretty good day. Why couldn't I get that day over and over...?

My life has spanned eight decades that have taken me all over the world and I never imagined anything like what we have experienced and will probably continue to experience for months — if not years — as the direct and collateral results of the malicious and irresponsible actions of the People's Republic of China. It is ludicrous to when you consider how vulnerable the world was. It doesn't matter whether the virus originated in a laboratory or in a filthy "wet market" where exotic live animals and seafood were sold. It is difficult not to be resentful toward the Chinese government — but it's easy to wake up and make sure that nothing like this ever happens again. America was too busy buying everything in sight, partying, doing drugs, posting selfies and pictures of other people's luxury cars on Facebook and Instagram, and doing everything we could to keep up with the Kardashians. We must take control of our lives now before we lose everything.

Many Americans might relate to these lyrics from *Against the Wind* (1980) by Bob Seger:

WASH YOUR HANDS

Guess I lost my way
There were oh-so many roads
I was living to run and running to live
Never worried about paying or even how much I
    owed
Moving eight miles a minute for months at a time
Breaking all of the rules that would bend
I began to find myself searching
Searching for shelter again and again

Some of us have taken advantage of the shutdown to reflect on our lives and — in some cases— reinvent ourselves. Others have allowed themselves to fall prey to the evil forces in America that would have us feel guilty for things that happened in America over which we had no effective control.

There are those who are advocating the complete "dismantling of America's political and economic system". The November 2020 election will, in many ways, determine the near-term and long-term future of America — and the world. Let's not give in to terrorists.

My strength during the pandemic has come from my belief in myself, in God, in the American system, and in the American people. And from my wife and daughter.

WASH YOUR HANDS

I have already shared my daughter Ali's email and she is an ongoing source of information, inspiration, and love.

The other Ali in my life — my wife — is the love of my life, my best friend, my partner, and my greatest source of strength. Every morning for many, many years she gives me the same speech that goes something like this:

"Work smart today — not hard. Remember who you are, and that God put you here on earth for a reason and gave you the ability to influence people. You change people's lives every day — you help make their dreams come true. Don't waste your time with sudor y pedos. Don't let anyone get you off the market. Stay BADASS. Trust your instincts. Be careful out there. I love you."

Please read my last book — *C19 Economics: Your Guide to Personal and Business Finance.* There are already too many financial guides on the market. And everyone is a "financial guru" — especially all of those newly licensed recruit drinking (and serving) the Kool-Aid at MLM meetings for all those get-rich-financial literacy clones whose 60 second speeches By now you probably know that you need help with your finances but

WASH YOUR HANDS

not know where to get it. If you live in California I might be able to help you. I have been advising people for over five decades.

The world of finance is very different than it was when I began in financial services more than fifty-five years ago. If you don't believe me watch a few episodes of *American Greed* and you will be asking yourself "how could those people be that stupid?" They were not just stupid — they were greedy. Markets are driven by FOMO — fear of missing out. Be bold, not greedy. *Audentes fortuna iuvat* means fortune favors the bold.

Within the pages of this book are everything you need to get started on your **Road to Millions** except what that little racehorse — Seabiscuit — had. Seabiscuit had **heart**. Heart is the "x-factor" that you combine with passion, desire, knowledge, experience, talent, and what "G's" call game to get the "cheese". Hopefully you have heart and we have given you enough information and inspiration to "bring home the bacon". Do not be afraid to be a "Capitalist pig" but keep in mind that greed is not always good. And like they say on Wall Street: "**Bulls** make money, **bears** make money, **pigs** get slaughtered."

WASH YOUR HANDS

The Beatles discovered backmasking — recording a message backwards onto a track to leave a hidden message — on their *Rubber Soul* album in 1965. So here is my hidden message that you do not have to play backwards but you do have to flip over:

I am honored and grateful that you have made it to the back of our book.
May your Road to Millions be adventurous, exciting, and successful.
Hold on tight to your dreams.
Reach for the stars — all of them.
Think creatively.
Color outside the lines.
And wash your hands for lunch.

INSPIRATION

Just don't give up trying to do what you really want to do. Where there is love and inspiration, I don't think you can go wrong.

— Ella Fitzgerald

Here in random order are sone of the books, poems, songs, and movies that have inspired me over the years. Please email yours to: RobertMillerNow@Gmail.com and I will add them to future editions of *Second Wind*.

<u>Books</u>

Siddhartha
 By Hermann Hesse

Think and Go Rich and Laws of Success
By Napoleon Hill

The Wonderful Wizard of Oz
By L. Frank Baum

The Little Prince
Wind, Sand and Stars
Night Flight
By Antoine de Saint-Exupéry

INSPIRATION

Books (continued)

Walden
Civil Disobedience
By Henry David Thoreau

Moby Dick
By Herman Melville

The Pearl
Grapes of Wrath
By John Steinbeck

The Great Gatsby
F. Scott Fitzgerald

1984
Animal Farm
George Orwell

Fahrenheit 451
Ray Bradbury

Start with Why
Simon Sinek

Screw Business as Usual
Richard Branson

Alice's Adventures in Wonderland
Lewis Carroll

INSPIRATION

Movies

The Wind and the Lion

A Man and a Woman

Chariots of Fire

Camelot

Grand Prix

Ground Hog Day

The Illusionist

The Greatest Showman

Wolf of Wall Street

Poems

Stopping by Woods on a Snowy Evening
By Robert Frost

Ulysses
By Alfred, Lloyd Tennyson

The Song of Hiawatha
By Henry Wadsworth Longfellow

If
By Rudyard Kipling

INSPIRATION

Songs

Running on Empty
Jackson Browne

Nineteenth Nervous Breakdown
Rolling Stones

American Tune
Kodachrome
Paul Simon

America
Sweet Caroline
Neil Diamond

Helter Skelter
Back in the USSR
All You Need is LOve
Beatles

We Are the Champions
Killer Queen
My Best Friend
Queen

American Pie
Don McLean

Dancing in the Dark
Rick Springfield

MY STORY

Whether I shall turn out to be the hero of my own life, or whether that station will be held by anybody else, these pages must show.

— Charles Dickens
David Copperfield

To help you change your story it might be valuable for you to know my story. In today's social climate I might be accused of having grown up with "white privilege" but I am not sure what that may or may not mean. I confess to being white but refuse to apologize for it —or for my actions or for those of any of my ancestors.

My ancestors came to America from the same part of the world at about the same time. My paternal ancestors sailed from London and landed in Boston in 1635. My maternal ancestors sailed from Barcelona to Baja California fifty years later. We are Americans who have spilled blood, sweat, and tears to make America great. And I am proud to be an American — even now.

MY STORY

A baby-boomer, I was born at the period of America's most amazing economic recovery after World War II. Unless you are part of my generation you will never understand those *Wonder Years* and *Happy Days*.

Our times are, perhaps, best described by the lines of Charles Dickens in *A Tale of Two Cities* written in 1859:

> It was the best of times, it was the worst of times, it was the age of wisdom, it was the age of foolishness, it was the epoch of belief, it was the epoch of Incredulity, it was the season of Light, it was the season of Darkness, it was the spring of hope, it was the winter of despair, we had everything before us, we were all going direct to Heaven, we were all going direct the other day…

Our parents, grandparents, and great-grandparents all struggled through the Great Depression. Those who survived the second world war had no idea what was in store for them in the Cold War. What they did know is they lost friends and family members and sacrificed to make "the world safe for democracy." They went without new tires and sugar too long.— and just not tires and sugar.

MY STORY

Almost everything was ration for the war effort — meat, nylons, candy bars, and almost everything. When the war ended and factories transitioned from making guns to butter we entered America's greatest era of consumerism.

The pent-up demand for goods and services catapulted our generation into an era of prosperity far beyond that which had been unimagined even by Wall Street and Madison Avenue. And that was how my childhood began.

We became a generation of greed and excess. We rode around in gas guzzling cars that had fins like spaceships. Women wore fur coats and men wore diamond rings. The middle class became wealthy as they tried to keep up with the Jones.

My parents bought their first house in Los Angeles for $5,000 (now worth $700,000), they paid $10,000 for their second house (now worth $2,000,000), and they paid $30,000 for their third house (no worth $1,500,000). I mention these houses so you can relate to the leverage of real estate. Those houses were all a part of their dreams.

MY STORY

We drove around in big cars to drive-in restaurants and drive-in movies. Growing up in Southern California we hung out in places many other people dreamed about — we lived the California Dream — and saw movie stars.

I experienced my wonder years at Malibu and in Hollywood and Beverly Hills. We went to Disneyland and Knott's Berry Farm as often as we wanted. My mother made sure that we had the biggest Easter Baskets from See's Candy and that we had new bicycles every year. She told us that our father could support us with his job at Douglas Aircraft but that she worked there night shift there so that we could have everything that she did not have growing up.

My mother was six years old when the Great Depression came along. It probably did not make much difference because her parents were already poor — extremely poor. My mother grew up in one room with the only water being in the pots that were placed under the table legs to keep spiders, rats, and cockroaches from crawling up on her at night. My grandparents crawled their way out of poverty in time to buy her a new 1940 Chevy convertible for her 16th birthday.

MY STORY

I am sharing this with you so that you can understand who I am and why. We are all a product of our back pages. These are mine.

My mother and her mother were both indelibly shaped by those years of poverty. And their lives were shaped in completely diverse ways.

My grandmother started out as a rich kid until she was a teenager and her father left her mother to marry his secretary. She ran away from home and married my grandfather —a illiterate ditch-digger with a second-grade education— at seventeen. She was barely eighteen when my mother was born, and she promised herself she and her daughter would not be poor for long.

An only child, my mother was given everything that her parents could sacrifice to provide — from orthodontic braces to orthopedic shoes. A lot changed during my mother's childhood as the little family literally went from extremely poor to wealthy middle-class.

My grandmother was a saver and bought her clothes at the Salvation Army and Goodwill her entire life. The only new clothes she wore

MY STORY

since childhood were the clothes she was buried in. She clipped coupons to buy groceries even though she had a safe deposit box with stocks and bonds with coupons to clip. Unfortunately my grandmother had a "poverty mentality" until she died.

My mother was the exact opposite. She wanted the best and the most of everything. She had a big heart but was wasteful and had no concept of money. She worked hard bit was a spender — not a saver.

As my wonder years evolved into my happy days and I took seriously the stories I was brought up on. I wanted more than the weekly allowance my father gave me for doing chores, so I became an entrepreneur at an early age. I cleaned apartments and made home repairs for my grandparents and our neighbors. I mowed lawns and sold magazines. I studied the stock market.

Looking back my happy days — my teenage years — were not that happy. My parents argued constantly and there was ongoing tension between my mother and her mother. My grandfather had died when I was nine years old and my mother became depressed.

MY STORY

I was there when my grandfather died, and it was a turning point in my life. My mother cried hysterically and kept repeating: "He's gone. I will never be able to tell him that I love him again. I'll never be able to give him a shirt for his birthday or give him a kiss." She kept saying the same thing repeatedly. That day impressed on my mind that nobody lives forever. And I eventually learned that I must do everything I can to live every day with passion and gratitude.

The years have passed quickly — one Cold War has ended and another one has begun. We have gone from one brief shining moment to a "season of darkness." Our economy and way of life are both under attack. I plan to do everything I can to help save both.

Someday I will write my autobiography titled "My Back Pages" and fill in the years between that day and now. All I will share now is that I grew up on the beaches of my native Southern California, have travelled around the world and am in love with my beautiful Colombian wife and her country. These are the most challenging times and crazier than I would have ever imagined. My story will be continued.

You gain strength, courage, and **confidence** *by every experience in which you really stop to look fear in the face. You are able to say to yourself, 'I lived through this horror. I can take the next thing that comes along.' You must do the thing you think you cannot do.*

Eleanor Roosevelt

My Books Available on Amazon

www.ingramcontent.com/pod-product-compliance
Lightning Source LLC
Chambersburg PA
CBHW070207100426
42743CB00013B/3078